How to Draw 30 Guns

The Step by Step Book to Draw 30 Different Guns

BY

Melody Love

© 2019 Melody Love All Rights Reserved

Copyright/License Page

No one is allowed to copy (print or electronic), republish, publish, distribute, sell and post it on social media sites without written confirmation from the author. If an illegal action is taken then the author has the legal rights to sue that person or company. If you have come across this book through illegal channels, delete it and if possible report it.

The author has taken every precaution so that the information in the book is educational, informational and true. But, the author is not responsible if something happens due to the actions of the readers.

Table of Contents

Introduction 6

SET 1 8

SET 2 14

SET 3 20

SET 4 26

SET 5 32

SET 6 38

SET 7 44

SET 8 50

SET 9 56

SET 10 62

SET 11 68

SET 12 74

SET 13 80

SET 14 86

SET 15 92

SET 16 98

SET 17 104

SET 18 110

SET 19 116

SET 20 122

SET 21 128

SET 22 134

SET 23 140

SET 24 146

SET 25 152

SET 26 158

SET 27 164

SET 28 170

SET 29 176

SET 30 182

Author's Afterthoughts 188

About the Author 189

Introduction

Why do parents beg their children to draw and color, even when they hate it? Because drawing is the best way to work on motor skills and coordination. This is a crucial part of every toddler and child's life. If these skills are not developed on time the child will have difficulties in school and everyday life.

Using this book to help your child build these skills will also help you get more time together and have some fun. Enjoy every minute with your child, see how he gets better and better as you work together with the help of this book. You will see that it is all about the simplicity of the drawing instruction. You can even have a type of competition. See who will draw and color the drawing better. This will test your child skills even more. Just don't forget to give him a chance, make a mistake on purpose. It will show him that making mistakes is not something to be afraid of. Mistakes should be seen as a chance to get better. He will soon understand that if he keeps trying and pushes forward he can achieve anything.

Draw and color the same thing a few times. But don't aim for perfection. Aim for something similar. Do you see changes in the drawing? Has your child drawn another item, like a flower and tree, etc.? Don't scold him over this. He is using his imagination and starts to draw better and better. Drawings are the best way to get your child to express their feelings.

Drawing can tell many things about your child. This is because it is the easiest way to express him, especially if he still doesn't have many words in his vocabulary. That is why a child with delayed speech need to focus on drawing too. It not only helps with eye coordination but also with expressing their feelings.

Drawing is truly a magical experience. So share it with your child. Use the drawings in this book to have fun and to teach him how valuable art is.

SET 1

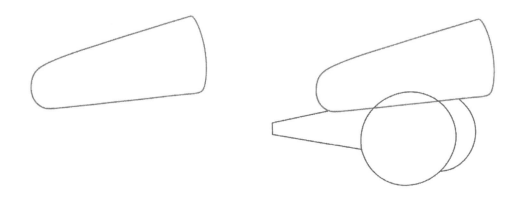

STEP 1　　　　　　　　STEP 2

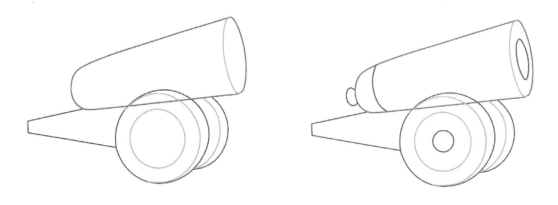

STEP 3　　　　　　　　STEP 4

1. Begin by drawing the cylinder shape that is shown in red.

2. That's right! Add the parts that appear in green onto the shape you just created.

3. Place the yellow circles onto your picture as shown in the example.

4. Very good! Copy the blue lines from the example onto your page.

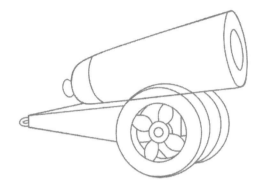

STEP 5

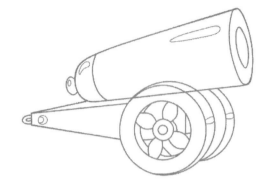

STEP 6

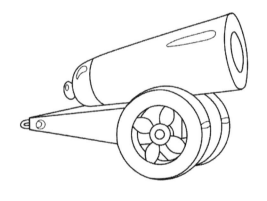

STEP 7

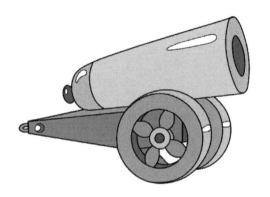

STEP 8

5. You're doing great! Add some detail to this drawing by copying the light blue lines from the example onto your picture. Don't worry if lines overlap, these will be fixed later.

6. That's perfect! Continue to copy the light blue lines onto your page to create all the smaller details. Take time to compare the images before moving on to ensure you haven't missed any of these important parts.

7. Keep going! Erase any lines that overlap and go over the outline in black to make it solid. You want your picture to match the sample image provided.

8. Amazing! You can now add some color to your drawing by looking at the example or choosing your own. Have fun with this step before moving on.

STEP 9   **STEP 10**

9. It is time to add shading to your drawing now. Shading is created by placing dark and light areas in various places to create depth and realness. Use the example to help you with this step and take your time.

10. You did an exceptional job drawing this picture! Feel free to design a background or add more detail. Don't forget, the more that you practice, the better you will become at drawing. Way to go!

SET 2

STEP 1   STEP 2

STEP 3   STEP 4

1. Draw a small, thin rectangle like the one shown in red.

2. Copy the green lines onto your page to create the handle of this gun.

3. Terrific! Add the yellow piece to your drawing.

4. Create the trigger by copying the blue lines.

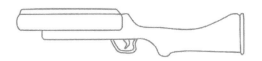

STEP 5

STEP 6

STEP 7

STEP 8

5. Awesome! Give the outline some shape by copying the light blue lines onto your page.

6. That's the way! Continue to use the light blue lines as a guide and create some small details on this image.

7. Good work! Go over the outline in black to make it solid and erase any unneeded lines.

8. Have some fun adding color to this picture. The example is there to inspire you, Get creative.

 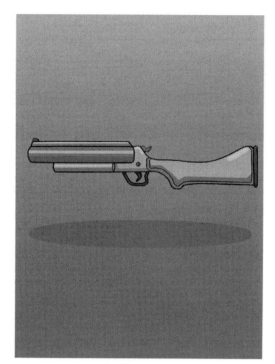

STEP 9 STEP 10

9. Wonderful! Now that you have color, it is time to add shading. Looking at the example, copy the darker areas of shading on to your page to create depth and mimic light. Take your time.

10. Wow, that is fantastic! Go ahead and give this picture a colorful background or add more detail. Remember to practice as much as possible to improve your skills. Good going!

SET 3

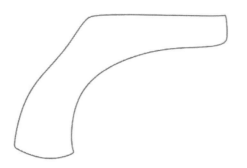

STEP 1

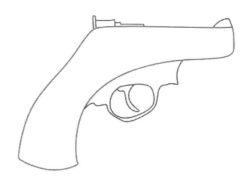

STEP 2

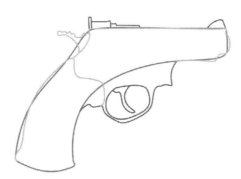

STEP 3

STEP 4

1. Using curved lines, create the shape that is shown in red.

2. Good! Now, add the green lines from the example onto your page.

3. Place the yellow parts on your picture as shown.

4. Terrific! Add the blue lines to your page by looking at the example provided.

STEP 5

STEP 6

STEP 7

STEP 8

5. Copy the light blue lines from the example to your page to create shape and detail around the edges.

6. That's great! Continue to copy the light blue lines to create all the smaller details. Take your time and compare the images to ensure you add all of these essential parts.

7. You're good at this! Go over the outline in black and erase any unneeded lines. You want your picture to look like the sample image provided.

8. Add a splash of color to your picture by copying the example or choosing your favorites.

STEP 9

STEP 10

9. Let's create shading for this image now! Shading will make your picture appear more realistic and is produced by placing darker and lighter areas in various places. Use the example as a guide to add shading to your drawing.

10. That is very impressive! Go ahead and add some color or detail to the background of your picture if you like. Remember, the more that you practice, the more natural drawing will become. Great job!

SET 4

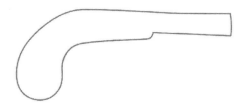

STEP 1

STEP 2

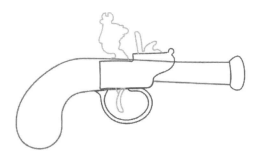

STEP 3

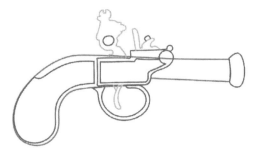

STEP 4

1. Copy the red lines onto your page as shown.

2. Place the green shapes into your picture by looking at the example.

3. Awesome! Add the yellow lines now.

4. Using the example for help, place the blue lines into your picture as displayed.

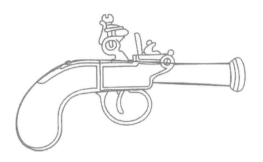
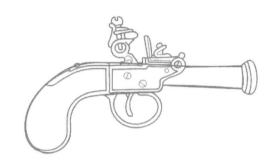

STEP 5 **STEP 6**

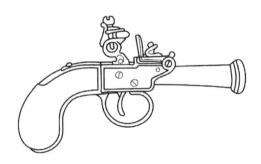
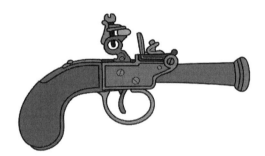

STEP 7 **STEP 8**

5. Keep up the good work! Add shape and detail to your drawing using the light blue lines as a guide.

6. Splendid! Keep adding all the details that appear in light blue.

7. Erase any unneeded lines and go over the edges in black to make the image solid.

8. Add color to your picture as shown.

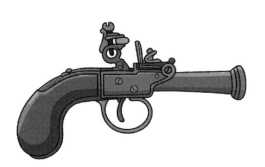

STEP 9

STEP 10

30

9. Create shading by making darker and light areas in various places. The example is there to help you with this step. Give it a try!

10. You did a fantastic job! Give your picture a unique background and add more shading. Don't forget to keep practicing, and your skills will improve. Way to go!

SET 5

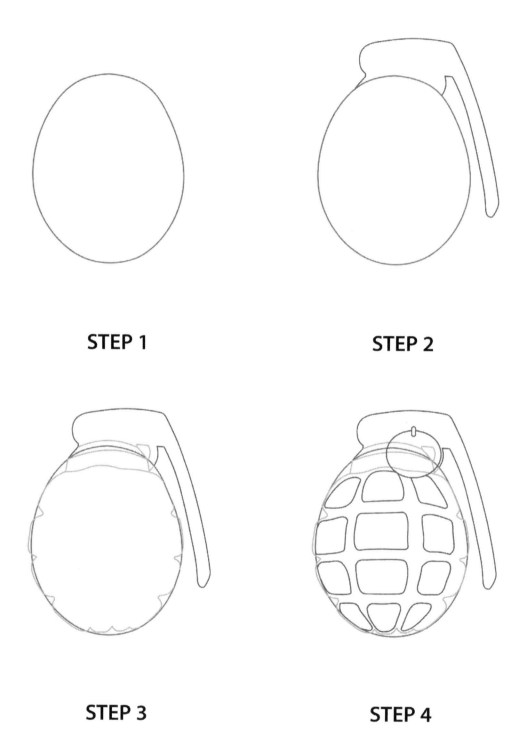

STEP 1

STEP 2

STEP 3

STEP 4

32

1. Draw a large circular shape like the one shown in red.

2. Copy the green lines onto your page.

3. Place the yellow lines onto your picture to begin adding some shape and detail.

4. The blue lines will help you add some of the smaller parts to this picture.

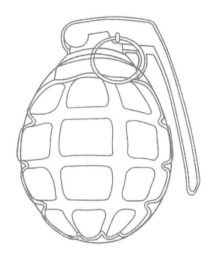

STEP 5

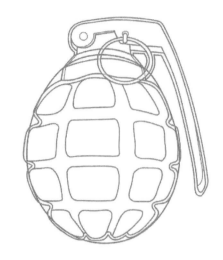

STEP 6

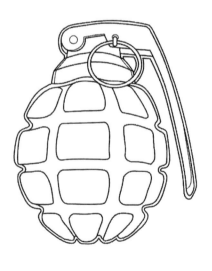

STEP 7

STEP 8

5. That is excellent! Copy the light blue lines from the example to begin adding shape to the outside of your image.

6. Keep going! Continue adding the light blue lines by looking carefully at the example provided.

7. You are doing an excellent job! Go over the outline in black to make it solid and fix up any small mistakes. Your drawing should look similar to the sample picture.

8. Give your picture a pop of color! You can copy the example or choose different colors. Have some fun with this step.

STEP 9

STEP 10

36

9. That's very artistic! Use the example to help you add shading to your picture now. Shading is created by placing dark and light areas in various places to mimic light. Try adding shading to your drawing as shown.

10. Very impressive! Feel free to design a unique background and add some more shading to your picture. Try to practice a little bit each and every day. Good going!

SET 6

STEP 1

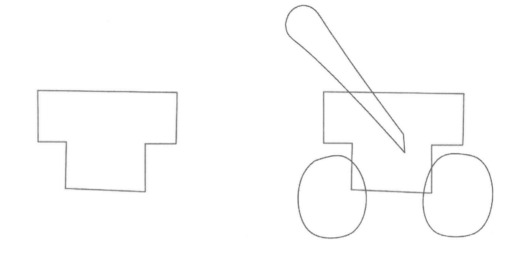

STEP 2

STEP 3

STEP 4

1. Use short, straight lines to create the shape that appears in red.

2. Nice! Add the parts shown in green onto the shape you just created. Remember, the example is there when you need guidance.

3. Look at the example and copy the yellow lines onto your page.

4. You've got it! Place the blue lines into your picture now.

STEP 5

STEP 6

STEP 7

STEP 8

5. Create shape and definition using the light blue lines as a guide.

6. Perfect! Keep adding the small details shown in light blue. Take your time and compare the pictures, so you don't miss any of these essential parts.

7. Go over the outline in black and erase any overlapping parts.

8. Have a bit of fun adding color to your picture. The example is there to give you ideas.

STEP 9

STEP 10

9. Now that you have color, it is time to add shading. Looking at the example carefully, copy the dark and light areas onto your page to imitate light and create depth.

10. You did a fabulous job drawing this picture! You can create a background or add more detail if you like. Don't forget, practice makes perfect, so keep it up!

SET 7

STEP 1

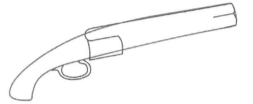

STEP 2

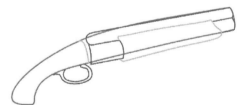

STEP 3

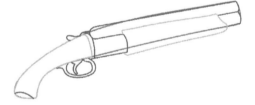

STEP 4

1. Begin by drawing the shape shown in red.

2. Add the pieces that appear in green.

3. Very good! Place the yellow lines onto your page.

4. Looking at the example, copy the lines that are drawn in blue.

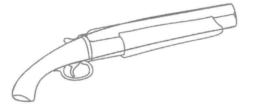
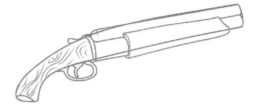

STEP 5

STEP 6

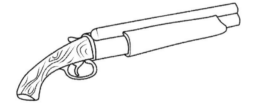

STEP 7

STEP 8

5. Right on! Give this picture some shape and detail by copying the light blue lines. Don't worry, the overlapping lines will be fixed later.

6. Nice job! Continue to add the light blue lines from the example onto your page to create the smaller details. Comparing the pictures will help during this step.

7. You are amazing! Go over the outline in black and erase any unneeded lines.

8. Color your picture the same as the example or choose your favorite colors.

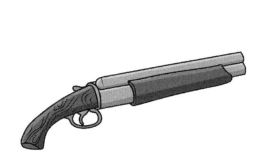
STEP 9

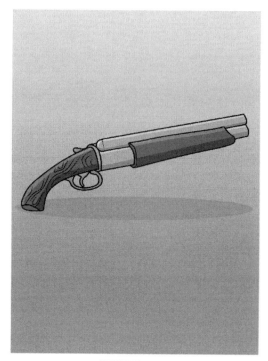
STEP 10

9. That's how it's done! Create shading by copying the light and dark areas from the example onto your picture. Take your time, shading will make your image more realistic.

10. Wow, you did a fantastic job! Give this drawing a background and add some extra detail. Remember to keep practicing as much as you can. Great work!

SET 8

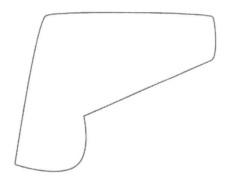

STEP 1

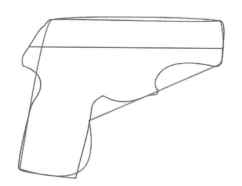

STEP 2

STEP 3

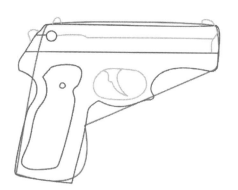

STEP 4

1. Copy the red lines onto your page from the example.

2. Great! Add the green lines to the shape you just created.

3. Place the yellow parts on your page as shown.

4. That's the way! Copy the blue lines now.

STEP 5

STEP 6

STEP 7

STEP 8

52

5. Start adding shape and detail to the edges using the light blue lines as a guide.

6. Fantastic work! Continue to copy the light blue lines from the example onto your page. Take your time and compare the two images before moving on.

7. You've got the hang of this! Go over the outline in black and erase any unneeded lines.

8. Take some time to add color to your picture. You can choose any colors you like or copy the ones used in the example.

STEP 9

STEP 10

9. Outstanding! Now that you have color, you will want to add shading to your picture. Shading is created by placing dark and light areas in various places. Use the example as a guide to complete this step.

10. That is extremely impressive! Give your drawing a distinct background and add more detail. Don't forget to practice often, and your skills will continue to improve. Good work!

SET 9

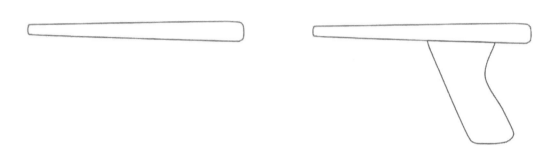

STEP 1　　　　　　　　STEP 2

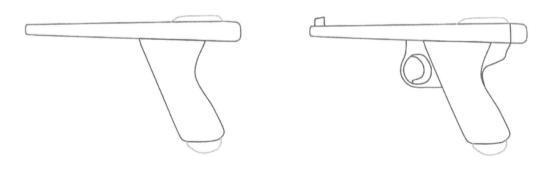

STEP 3　　　　　　　　STEP 4

1. Create the shape that is shown in red.

2. Use the green lines to build the handle of this gun.

3. Excellent! Copy the small pieces that appear in orange and yellow.

4. Add the blue lines to your picture now.

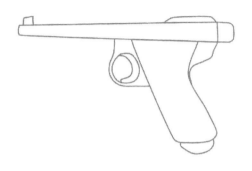

STEP 5

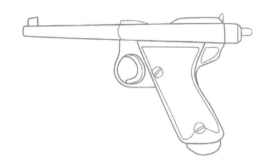

STEP 6

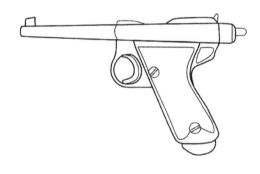

STEP 7

STEP 8

5. That's wonderful! Give shape and detail to the edges by adding the light blue lines to your page. Don't worry if lines overlap, these will be fixed shortly.

6. You're talented! Continue to add the light blue lines to your picture from the example. Remember to compare the images to ensure you haven't missed any parts.

7. Erase any overlapping lines and go over the edges in black.

8. Have fun coloring your picture any way you want.

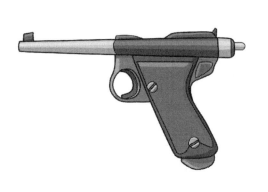

STEP 9

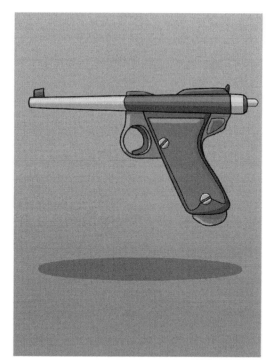

STEP 10

9. Looking closely at the example provided, copy the light and dark areas of shading to your page to make your picture more 3D.

10. You have improved a lot! Feel free to design a background and add extra detail. Keep up the excellent work and keep practicing!

SET 10

STEP 1　　　　　　　　　STEP 2

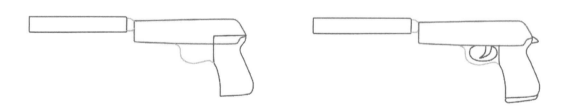

STEP 3　　　　　　　　　STEP 4

1. Begin by copying the red lines to your page.

2. That's exactly right! Place the green shapes onto your picture now.

3. Perfect! Copy the yellow lines to complete this step.

4. Awesome! Insert the pieces that appear in blue into your picture.

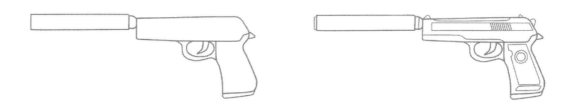

STEP 5   STEP 6

STEP 7   STEP 8

5. You're doing great! Create some shape and detail using the light blue lines.

6. Keep going! Carry on with adding all the light blue lines to your picture to create detail. The example is there to guide you; compare it with your drawing when you need help.

7. Go over the edges in black to make the image solid and erase any unneeded lines now. Your drawing should look similar to the sample image provided before you move on.

8. Get creative and design your picture with your favorite colors.

STEP 9

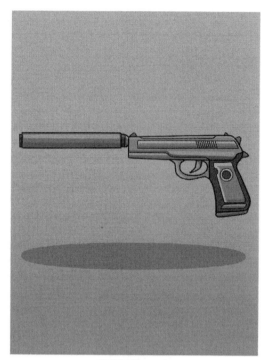

STEP 10

9. Create shading by copying the lighter and darker areas from the example onto your drawing as shown. Take your time, there are a lot of small shadows to add to this gun.

10. You did it! Go ahead and add detail or create a background for this image. Remember, the more that you practice, the better you will become. Keep it up!

SET 11

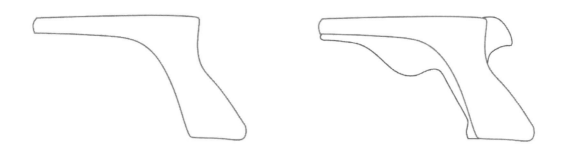

STEP 1 STEP 2

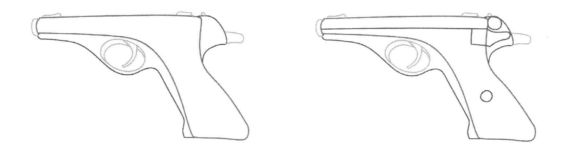

STEP 3 STEP 4

1. Recreate the shape that appears in red.

2. Use curved lines to add the parts that are shown in green.

3. That's flawless! Place the yellow lines into your picture now.

4. Add the pieces that appear in blue. Be sure to look at the example closely, so you don't miss anything.

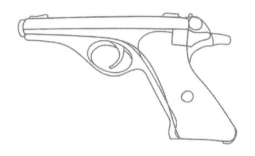

STEP 5

STEP 6

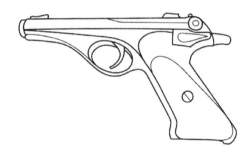

STEP 7

STEP 8

5. You're getting there! Give the outline shape and detail using the light blue lines.

6. Right on! Continue to copy the light blue lines to create all the small details. Don't forget to compare the images before moving on.

7. Erase any lines that overlap and go over the edges in black to make them solid.

8. Have a blast coloring this picture any way you wish or copy the colors used in the example.

STEP 9

STEP 10

9. Picture-perfect! Carefully add shading to this image using the example as a guide.

10. You should be very proud! Design a colorful background and add more shading to your picture. Try to practice as much as you can, and you may be a professional artist one day. Exceptional effort!

SET 12

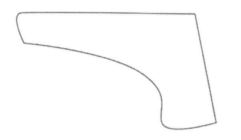

STEP 1

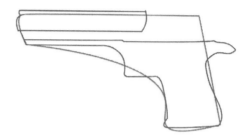

STEP 2

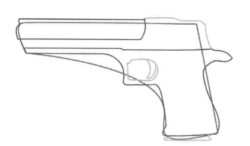

STEP 3

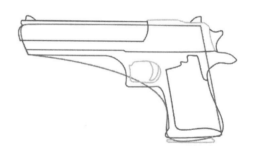

STEP 4

1. Draw the red shape to start.

2. Add the green lines onto the shape you created previously.

3. Nice going! Copy the yellow lines onto your page.

4. Add the pieces that are shown in blue to your picture from the example.

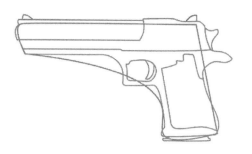

STEP 5

STEP 6

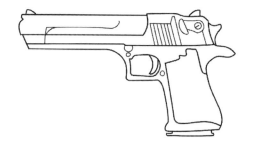

STEP 7

STEP 8

5. You've got it! Create shape by copying the light blue lines. Don't rush, there are a lot of parts to add here.

6. Very good! Continue to add the light blue lines onto your page from the example. Be sure to compare the images, so you don't miss any of these essential parts.

7. Go over the edges in black and erase any overlapping lines.

8. Have fun adding color! You can choose any colors you like or copy the example image provided.

STEP 9

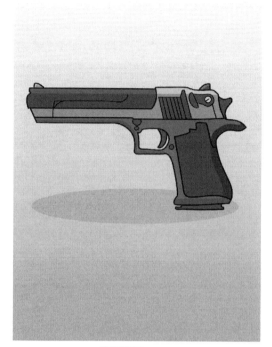

STEP 10

9. Take your time adding shading to this drawing by copying the darker and lighter areas as they appear in the example.

10. Way to go! Give this image a unique background and add more detail. Don't forget, practice make perfect. Well done!

SET 13

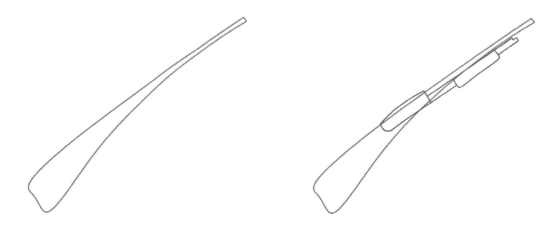

STEP 1 STEP 2

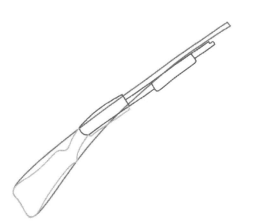 

STEP 3　　　　　　　　STEP 4

1. Start by copying the shape shown in red.

2. Now, add the parts that appear in green.

3. Super! Place the yellow lines into your picture as shown.

4. Copy the blue lines from the example to your drawing.

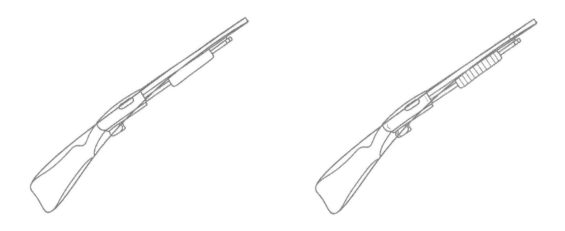

STEP 5   STEP 6

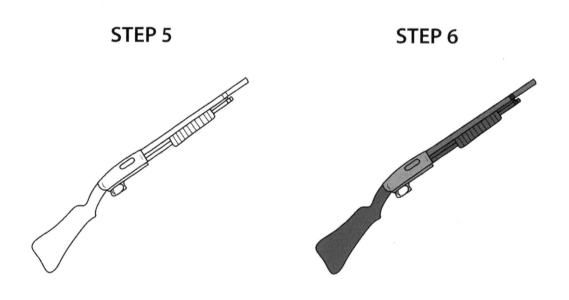

STEP 7   STEP 8

5. Neat! Build shape and definition by copying the light blue lines onto your page. Don't worry, the overlapping lines will be erased shortly. For now, just focus on adding them all to your picture.

6. That looks good! Continue to copy the light blue lines to add all the smaller details to this drawing. It helps to compare the two images.

7. You're doing a terrific job! Erase any unneeded lines and go over the outside of the image in black.

8. Design this gun using any colors you wish or copy the example provided. Have some fun with this step.

STEP 9

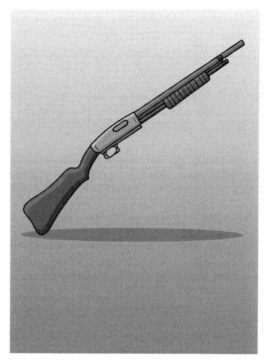

STEP 10

9. Very creative! Looking at the example, copy the areas of shading to your page as shown. Take your time, you don't want to miss any of these important shadows.

10. Tremendous! Give your picture a colorful background and add to the shading. Keep practicing your skills.

SET 14

STEP 1

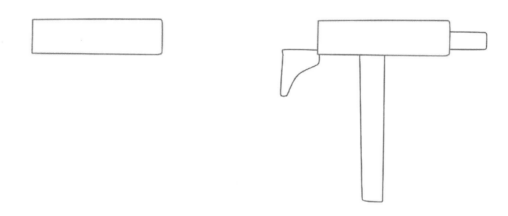

STEP 2

STEP 3

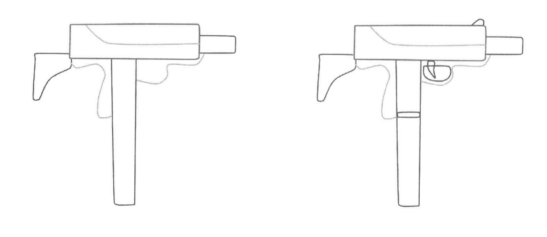

STEP 4

1. Begin by drawing a rectangle like the one shown in red.

2. Add the pieces shown in green onto the shape you just created.

3. Splendid! Place the yellow lines onto your picture as shown.

4. Copy the blue lines to your page now.

STEP 5

STEP 6

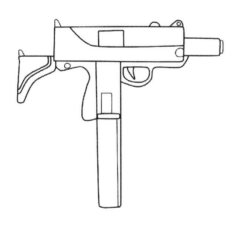

STEP 7

STEP 8

5. Great! Give your drawing some shape and detail using the light blue lines as a guide.

6. You've got this under control! Continue to copy the light blue lines from the example onto your picture.

7. You're a natural artist! Erase any lines that overlap and go over the edges in black to create one solid piece.

8. Add a pop of color to your picture!

STEP 9

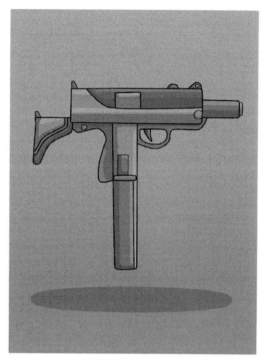

STEP 10

9. That's perfect! Look at the example carefully and copy the areas of shading to your page as shown. Take your time, there is a lot of shading to add to this image.

10. That's the way to do it! Give this drawing a creative background and add more detail. Remember to keep practicing, and you will get better each time. Good for you

SET 15

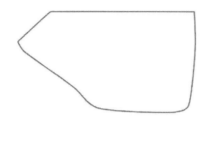

STEP 1

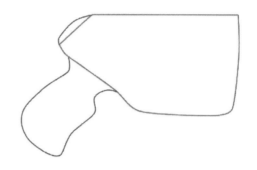

STEP 2

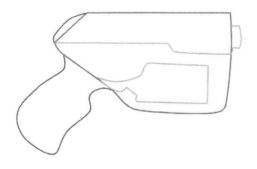

STEP 3

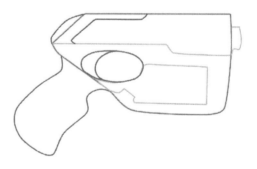

STEP 4

1. Begin by replicating the shape that is shown in red.

2. Create a handle by copying the green lines.

3. That's the way! Add the yellow lines onto your picture now.

4. Copy the shapes that appear in blue.

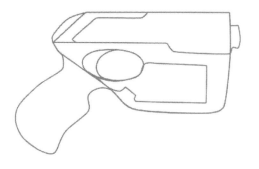
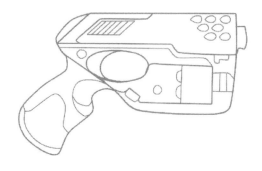

STEP 5

STEP 6

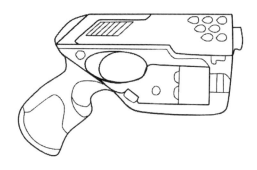

STEP 7

STEP 8

5. You've got it! Give the outline shape and detail by following the light blue lines in the example.

6. Perfect! Continue to copy the light blue lines to add some small details to this weapon.

7. Impressive work! Go over the outline in black to make it one solid piece and erase any unneeded lines.

8. Give this gun a bit of color. You can copy the example or choose your favorites. Have fun with this step.

STEP 9 **STEP 10**

9. Now that you have added color, it is time to create shading. Shading is made by placing dark and light areas in various places. Use the example to help you add shading to your picture.

10. You did a fabulous job drawing this gun! Go ahead and draw a background or add some extra detail. Don't forget to practice as much as you can. Way to go!

SET 16

STEP 1   STEP 2

STEP 3   STEP 4

1. Draw the rectangular shape shown in red.

2. Copy the green lines to create the handle.

3. Add the parts that appear in yellow.

4. Very good! Place the blue lines onto your picture.

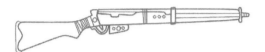

STEP 5 STEP 6

STEP 7 STEP 8

5. Give the edges some shape and detail using the light blue lines.

6. You're a natural! Continue to copy the light blue lines from the example onto your page as shown. Take your time, these details are essential.

7. Go over the outline in black and erase any unneeded lines. Your picture should look like the example before you move on.

8. It is time to add color! Feel free to choose any colors you wish or copy the example provided.

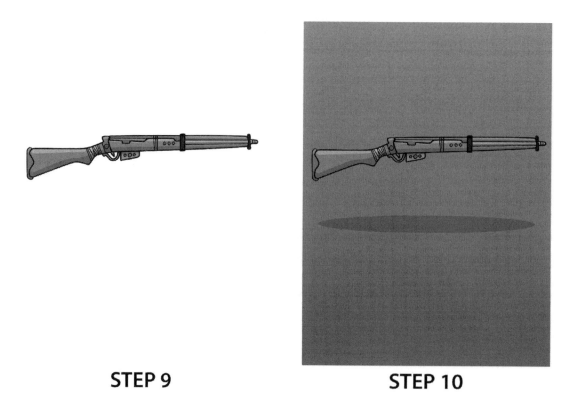

STEP 9   **STEP 10**

9. That's great! Create shading by placing dark and light areas on your image, as shown in the example. Don't rush this step, it will make your picture look more realistic.

10. You did a fantastic job! Add a colorful background and more shading. Remember, the more you practice, the better you will become at drawing. Good work!

SET 17

STEP 1

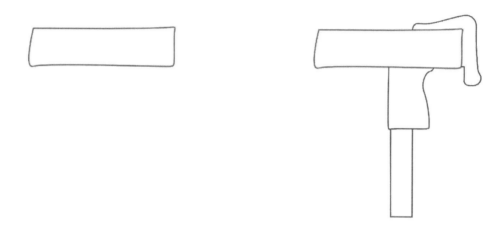

STEP 2

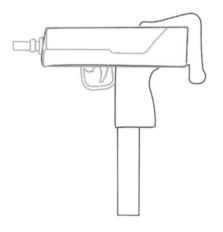

STEP 3

STEP 4

1. Draw a rectangle at the top of your page. This step appears in red on the example.

2. Copy the green lines on to your page from the sample.

3. Spectacular! Place the yellow pieces onto your picture as shown.

4. Add the small blue shapes to your image to begin adding detail.

STEP 5

STEP 6

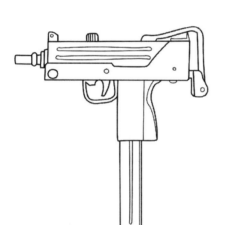

STEP 7

STEP 8

5. That's exactly right! Using the light blue lines as a guide, begin to create shape and detail around the edges of this image.

6. Continue to copy the light blue lines to your page to create all the small details that will make this picture look real. Compare the two images to ensure you have added all of these vital parts before moving on.

7. Excellent work! You may erase any overlapping lines and go over the edges in black. The goal is to have your drawing match the example provided.

8. Take some time to color your picture any way you wish or copy the example image. Have some fun with this step and don't be afraid to get creative.

STEP 9

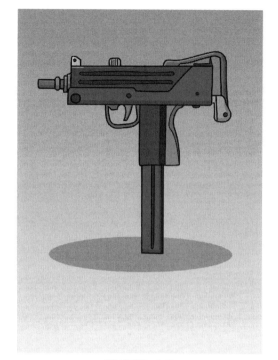

STEP 10

9. That looks great! Looking at the example for guidance, copy the areas of shading to your page as shown. Take your time, shading will make your drawing look more 3D and realistic.

10. You are outstanding! Give your picture a unique background and add more detail. Don't forget to keep practicing. Very good!

SET 18

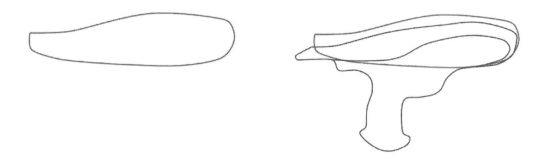

STEP 1　　　　　　　　STEP 2

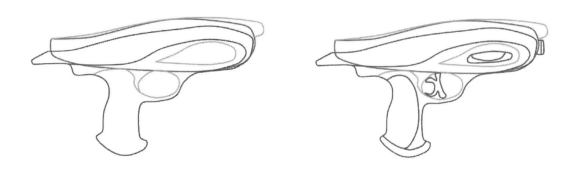

STEP 3　　　　　　　　STEP 4

1. Use curved lines to recreate the red shape.

2. Add the green lines onto the shape you just created by looking at the example provided.

3. Nice! Place the yellow lines onto your picture.

4. Copy the blue lines to your page now.

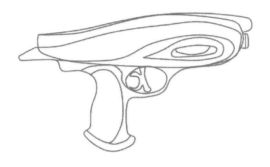
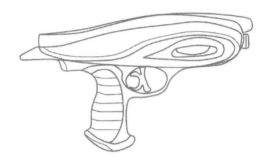

STEP 5   **STEP 6**

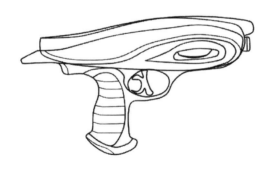

STEP 7   **STEP 8**

5. You're on a roll, keep it up! Create shape and definition around the edges of this image by copying the light blue lines. Take your time, and don't worry about lines overlapping.

6. Continue to copy all the light blue lines to your page. These lines will help you create all the small details that will make this picture look real. It helps to compare the images to ensure you don't miss anything.

7. That is the way to do it! Go over the outline in black to make it solid and erase any unneeded lines.

8. Go ahead and give this image some color! The example is there if you need inspiration.

STEP 9

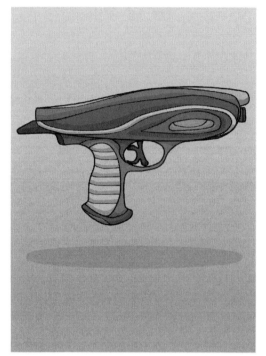

STEP 10

9. Very artistic! Looking closely at the example provided, add shading to your picture as shown. Don't rush this step, it is imperative.

10. Your picture looks great! Add a fun background color and more shading. Try to practice a little bit each day, and your skills will quickly improve. Good job!

SET 19

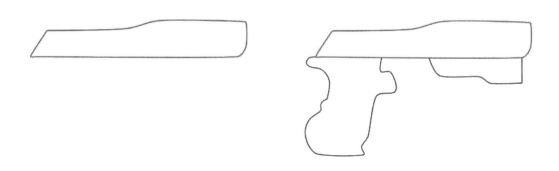

STEP 1   STEP 2

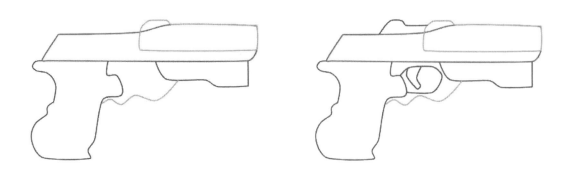

STEP 3   STEP 4

1. Recreate the shape shown in red.

2. Add the lines that appear in green.

3. Beautifully done! Copy the yellow parts to your page now.

4. Include the shapes that are shown in blue.

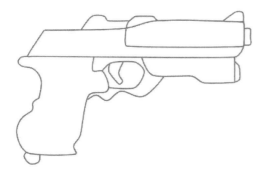

STEP 5

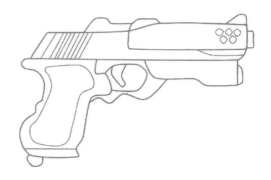

STEP 6

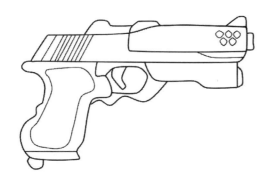

STEP 7

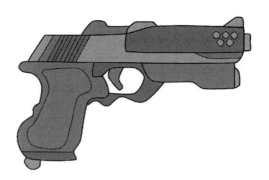

STEP 8

5. Give the edges some shape by copying the light blue lines to your page as shown. Don't worry, any overlapping lines will be erased later.

6. Terrific! Start adding the smaller details using the light blue lines as a guide. Be sure to compare the images to ensure you don't miss anything.

7. Go ahead and erase any overlapping lines and go over the edges in black to make them solid.

8. Get creative! Color your picture as shown, or choose your favorite colors.

STEP 9

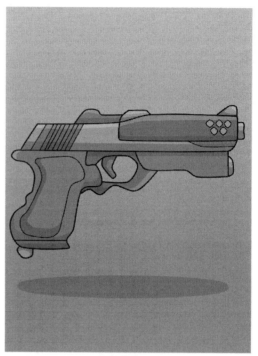

STEP 10

120

9. Now that you have added color copy the areas of shading shown in the example onto your page. This will help to make your drawing appear more realistic, so take your time.

10. That is the best one yet! Go ahead and design a background or draw more detail. Don't forget to practice often. Way to go!

SET 20

STEP 1

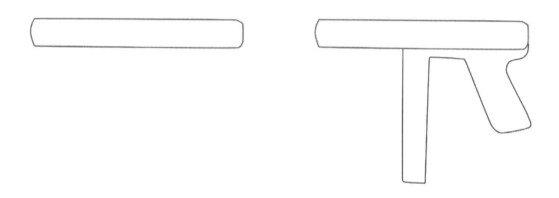

STEP 2

STEP 3

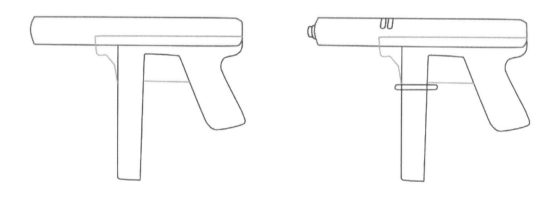

STEP 4

1. Create the shape shown in red.

2. Add the green lines from the example onto the shape you created previously.

3. Nice work! Add the yellow lines to your picture as shown.

4. Copy the pieces that appear in blue.

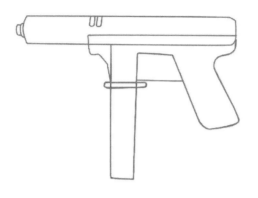

STEP 5

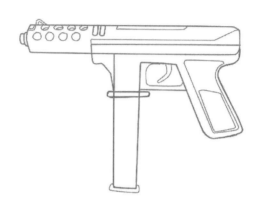

STEP 6

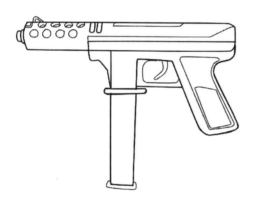

STEP 7

STEP 8

5. You've got the hang of this! Create shape and definition by copying the light blue lines to your page.

6. Super! Create all of the small details for this image using the light blue lines for help.

7. Very impressive! Erase any lines that overlap and go over the outline in black. Your drawing should look similar to the example provided before you move on.

8. Have some fun adding color to your drawing. You can copy the example image or choose your favorite colors. Using more than one color will help to make the image stand out.

STEP 9

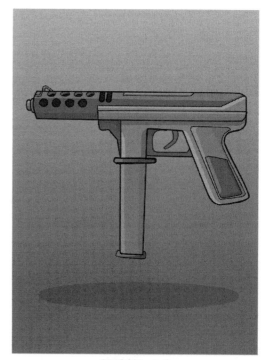

STEP 10

9. That is amazing! Carefully add the areas of shading shown in the example onto your page.

10. Way to go! You can add a background to your drawing or create more detail. Keep up the excellent work, and don't forget to keep practicing.

SET 21

STEP 1 STEP 2

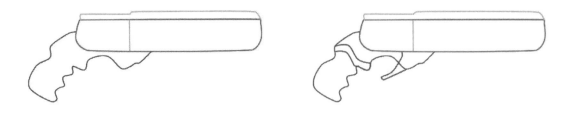

STEP 3 STEP 4

1. Begin by placing the red shape on your page.

2. Very good! Add the green lines to the shape you just created.

3. Using straight lines, add the parts that appear in yellow.

4. Copy the blue lines onto your picture now.

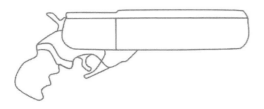

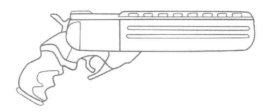

STEP 5

STEP 6

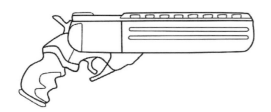

STEP 7

STEP 8

5. That's fantastic! Create shape along the outline by copying the light blue lines to your page as shown.

6. Keep going! Continue to copy the light blue lines from the example onto your drawing. Take your time, the small details in this step are vital.

7. Nicely done! Erase any lines that overlap and make the edges black.

8. Go wild with color! You can choose any colors you like or copy the ones shown in the example. Have fun with this step.

STEP 9

STEP 10

132

9. That is very creative! For this step you will copy the darker areas of shading from the example onto your page. Take your time, you don't want to miss any of these essential shadows.

10. You did an excellent job drawing this gun! Go ahead and give your picture a unique background. Remember, the best way to build your skills is through practice. Good going!

SET 22

STEP 1　　　　　　　　STEP 2

STEP 3　　　　　　　　STEP 4

1. Start by drawing a small, thin rectangle at the top of the page.

2. Add more rectangles by looking at the green lines.

3. Great! Copy the yellow lines to your picture as shown.

4. Place the blue lines on your page now.

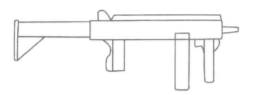
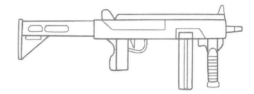

STEP 5					STEP 6

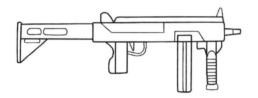

STEP 7					STEP 8

5. Outstanding! Begin adding some shape and detail using the light blue lines as a guide.

6. Amazing! Continue to add the light blue lines from the example onto your picture as shown. Compare the images to ensure you have added all of these critical parts.

7. Erase any unneeded lines and go over the edges in black to make them solid.

8. It is time to add color! You can copy the example or choose your favorite colors. Have fun with this step before moving on.

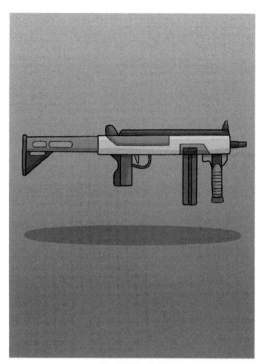

STEP 9 **STEP 10**

9. That's a work of art! Very carefully copy the darker areas of shading to your page from the example.

10. You should be proud! Give this drawing a distinct background and add more detail. Remember, practice makes perfect, so keep it up!

SET 23

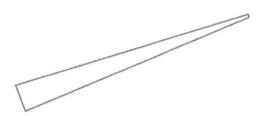
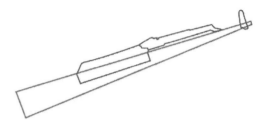

STEP 1   STEP 2

STEP 3   STEP 4

1. Draw the shape that appears in red.

2. Add the pieces that are shown in green.

3. Place the yellow lines onto your page.

4. Terrific! Attach the parts that appear in blue.

STEP 5

STEP 6

STEP 7

STEP 8

5. Give the edges some shape using the light blue lines for guidance.

6. That's right! Continue to copy the light blue lines from the example to your page to create detail. It's a good idea to compare the pictures before you move on.

7. Erase any lines that overlap and make the outline black.

8. You're on a roll! Add color to your picture as shown or choose any colors you wish.

STEP 9

STEP 10

9. Use shading to create depth by copying the darker areas from the example onto your page.

10. That looks perfect! Go ahead and design a background for this image and don't forget to keep practicing. Good job!

SET 24

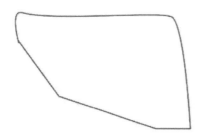

STEP 1

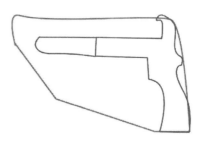

STEP 2

STEP 3

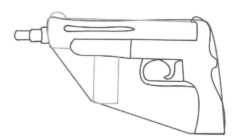

STEP 4

146

1. To start, draw the shape shown in red.

2. Place the green shapes into the shape you previously created. The example is there if you need help.

3. Good! Add the yellow lines to your picture as shown.

4. Place the blue pieces onto your picture now.

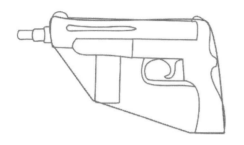

STEP 5   STEP 6

STEP 7   STEP 8

5. Create shape and detail by copying the light blue lines. Don't worry about extra or overlapping lines, these will be erased shortly.

6. Continue to add the light blue lines from the example onto your page as shown. Take a moment to compare the pictures before you move on.

7. You're doing well! Erase any extra lines and go over the outline in black to create one solid piece.

8. Have some fun coloring your picture. The example is there to give you ideas, or you can copy those colors to your page if you prefer.

STEP 9

STEP 10

150

9. Great! Now that you have added color, you can take time to add shading to your picture. Shading is made by placing darker areas in various places and helps your drawing look real. The example is there to guide you through this step, give it a try.

10. You did a fantastic job! Give your image a background and add some extra details. Remember to keep up the great work and keep practicing. Way to go!

SET 25

STEP 1   STEP 2

STEP 3   STEP 4

1. Place the red shape onto your page to begin.

2. Add the green lines from the example onto your page.

3. Right on! Copy the yellow lines to your picture now.

4. Look at the example and copy the blue lines to your page.

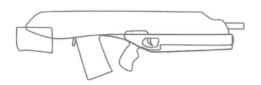

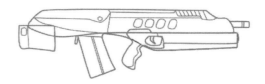

STEP 5

STEP 6

STEP 7

STEP 8

5. Create shape by copying the light blue lines.

6. Nice! Continue to copy the light blue lines to create all of the small details for this image.

7. You are really good at this! Go over the outline in black to make it one solid piece and erase any extra lines.

8. Take some time to color your picture any way you wish.

STEP 9

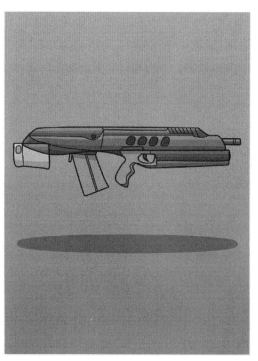

STEP 10

9. Using the example as a guide, create shading in various place to create realness and add dimension.

10. That's the way it's done! Feel free to add a background or create more detail. Remember, the more that you practice, the better you will become at drawing. Nice work!

SET 26

STEP 1

STEP 2

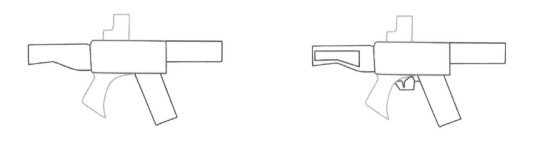

STEP 3

STEP 4

1. Draw a small rectangle close to the center of the page.

2. Add the parts that are shown in green on the example.

3. Now add the yellow shapes to your picture.

4. Place the small pieces that appear in blue onto your page as shown.

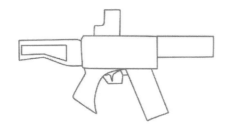

STEP 5

STEP 6

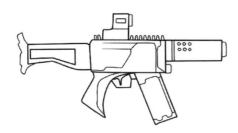

STEP 7

STEP 8

5. That's excellent! Give the edges some definition by copying the light blue lines to your page.

6. Perfect! Create detail by looking at the light blue lines in the example. Take your time and compare the two images to ensure you have added all of these small parts.

7. Superb work so far! Go over the edges with black to make them solid and erase any overlapping lines.

8. Give this picture a pop of color using the example for inspiration.

STEP 9

STEP 10

9. Nicely done! It is time to add shading to this image. Create shading by placing darker areas in various places. Look at the example for guidance.

10. You are very talented! Draw a background for this picture and create some extra detail. Keep up the great work and keep practicing as much as possible. Good job!

SET 27

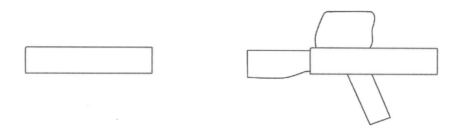

STEP 1   STEP 2

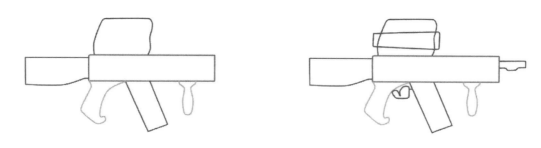

STEP 3   STEP 4

1. Draw a rectangle like the one shown in red.

2. Add the parts that appear in green.

3. Very good! Copy the yellow lines to your page now.

4. Excellent! Add the blue pieces to your picture as shown.

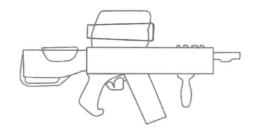

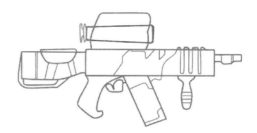

STEP 5

STEP 6

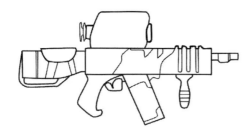

STEP 7

STEP 8

5. That's the way! Begin adding shape and detail using the light blue lines.

6. Perfect! Keep adding the light blue lines from the example onto your page.

7. Erase any unneeded or overlapping lines and go over the edges in black.

8. Color your picture as shown, or choose your favorite colors. Have fun with this step.

STEP 9

STEP 10

9. Look at the example and copy the areas of shading to your image as shown. This step is essential because it helps to create depth and mimic light. Take your time.

10. That is spectacular! Give this drawing a distinct background and add more detail. Don't forget, practice makes perfect. Keep up the excellent work!

SET 28

STEP 1   STEP 2

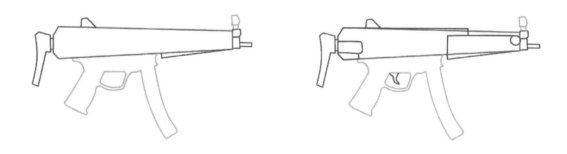

STEP 3   STEP 4

1. Start by recreating the shapes shown in red.

2. Good! Now add the parts shown in green.

3. That's right! Copy the yellow lines to your page to create the handle of this gun.

4. Place the blue piece onto your picture by looking at the example.

STEP 5

STEP 6

STEP 7

STEP 8

5. Using the light blue lines for help, start to add shape and definition to your picture as shown. Don't worry about lines overlapping, these will be fixed later.

6. Nice job! Keep copying the light blue lines to create all the small details for this drawing. Don't rush, these little pieces are essential.

7. You are doing awesome! Erase any overlapping lines and make the edges black to create one solid piece.

8. Great work, let's add color! You can copy the example provided or choose your favorite colors. Have a bit of fun with this step and feel free to get creative.

STEP 9

STEP 10

9. Excellent! Now that you have color take time to place shading on your picture. Shading is made by placing darker areas in various places to mimic light. The example is there to help you add shading to your image, go ahead.

10. That is absolutely amazing! Feel free to create a background and add more detail for this drawing. Try to practice each and every day to improve your drawing skills. Good going!

SET 29

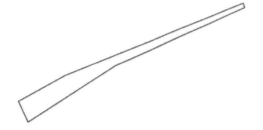

STEP 1

STEP 2

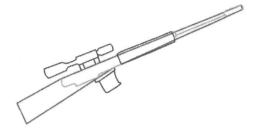

STEP 3

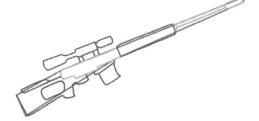

STEP 4

1. Use straight lines to create the shape shown in red.

2. Add the parts that appear in green onto the shape you just created. Remember, the example is there if you need it.

3. Place the yellow lines onto your picture.

4. Copy the blue lines to your page as shown.

STEP 5

STEP 6

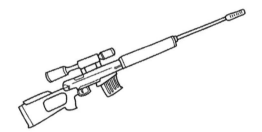

STEP 7

STEP 8

5. You've got it! Create shape and definition using the light blue lines.

6. Beautiful! Continue to add the light blue lines to your page as shown. Be sure to compare the pictures, so you don't miss any of these crucial pieces.

7. You have just about mastered this! Go over the edges in black to make them solid and erase any unneeded lines.

8. Get creative with color!

STEP 9

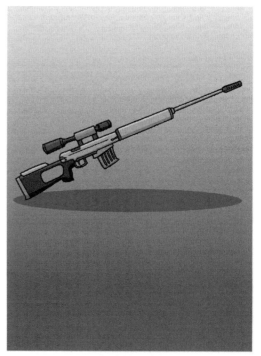

STEP 10

9. Add shading to your picture by carefully looking at the example and copying the darker areas as they appear.

10. You did a great job on this image! Add a pop of color and more shading. Don't forget, the more that you practice, the more natural drawing will get. Keep it up!

SET 30

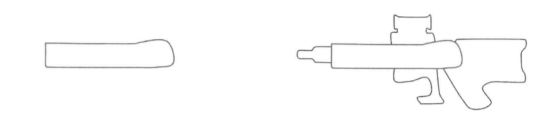

STEP 1 STEP 2

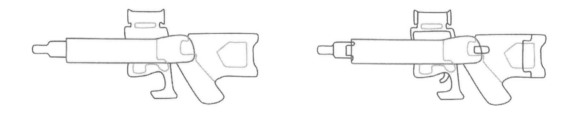

STEP 3 STEP 4

1. Draw the shape that is displayed in red.

2. Great! Add the parts that appear in green.

3. Place the yellow lines onto your page.

4. Now, copy the shapes that are shown in blue.

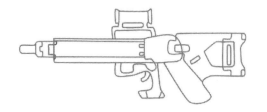

STEP 5

STEP 6

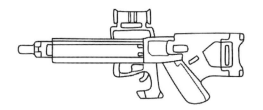

STEP 7

STEP 8

5. Terrific! Use the light blue lines to begin adding detail to your drawing. Take your time, there are a lot of small parts to add to this picture.

6. Very good! Keep adding the parts that appear in light blue onto your drawing as shown. Remember to compare the images to ensure you have added all these essential parts.

7. Erase any lines that overlap and make the edges black. Your drawing should match the example image provided.

8. It is time to add color! You can choose your favorite colors or copy the ones used in the example. Have a bit of fun with this step!

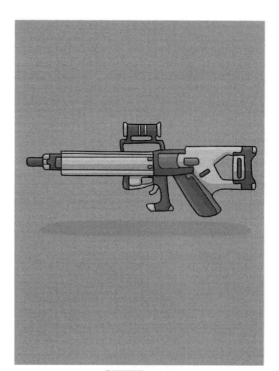

STEP 9　　　　　　　　STEP 10

9. Fabulous! Let's add shading to your picture now. Shading is created by placing darker areas in various places to mimic light. Use the example to help you place shading on your drawing.

10. You are on your way to becoming a professional artist! Give this picture a colorful background and add some extra details. Remember to practice as often as possible, and your skills will continue to improve. Way to go, you did it!

Author's Afterthoughts

Thank you for buying this book. As an author, I am so happy that you had the chance to learn from my book. There is no better feeling than knowing that I have helped someone to learn something new.

From so many books out there you still chose mine. It means you took your time to make the right decision and I am grateful for this. I am sure that you will learn from this book like never before.

What do you think about my book? Every feedback is welcomed. I consider honest feedbacks as my friends because they help me to grow to become even better. Your words will also inspire others too.

Have a great day

Melody Love

About the Author

Melody Love is born with a talent that many people pursue to build trough learning. Since she was a kid she showed promising drawing skills that her parents didn't ignore. They helped her get those skills trained and give her the push to become a world-known artist. In college, she already has drawn many paintings that were sold for a very good price. After she made enough money on her own, through selling her paintings she opened up gallery.

But there was something missing in her life. She wanted to help children and adults to learn how to draw. But not trough lessons like most art professors give, but simple step-by-step instructions.

Her books are fun and interesting, and that is why it inspires children from a young age to focus on their drawing and coloring skills. After she published her first couple of books she started receiving emails from parents grateful for helping their children fall in love with art.

She continues working on her paintings but also on new books. Right now she has more than a couple of books published and there are always more on the way. So, get her books and start having fun with your child. You will see amazing success after practicing with her books. Soon, your child will start to draw from his imagination, and he will start to make drawings that you will be surprised by.

Made in the USA
Middletown, DE
16 July 2021